The Scheming of Morgan Le Fay

by Simon Cheshire

Illustrated by Mark Oldroyd

CAST

Narrator

Arthur
King of England

Sir Accolon
loyal friend to
King Arthur

Morgan le Fay

half-sister to

King Arthur

Morgan's servant

Merlin

a magician

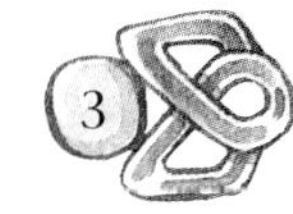

SCENE ONE

A misty woodland, beside a lake. Enter King Arthur, armed with Excalibur, and Sir Accolon. They are laughing together.

Narrator *One day, out on a hunting expedition, King Arthur and his trusted friend, Sir Accolon, have strayed far from the walls of Camelot. They have not caught a single deer, and their search has now led them away from any place they know.*

Accolon I swear to you, my lord, we passed this way less than an hour ago. Look, there is the lake!

Arthur Nonsense, Sir Accolon! This must be ... a second lake!

Accolon A second lake identical to the first? We are lost, sire! Admit it.

Arthur Hmm, it seems I must. I am glad we are far from Camelot. It would grieve me to have the court knowing that even I can lose my way.

Accolon *(laughing)* My lips are sealed, my lord. I warrant even Merlin could not find us in these dark and shrouded woods.

Narrator *At the mention of his name, Merlin appears before them as a ghostly presence.*

Merlin Who calls upon me? I am busy, high in the towers of Camelot, and should not be disturbed.

Arthur Our humblest apologies, Merlin. We find ourselves far from home, and missing your wise council, that is all.

Merlin If it is advice you seek, Arthur, then I must warn you to be on your guard. Your half-sister, Morgan le Fay, walks abroad. She wishes to take your place and be Queen. She can no more be trusted than a cobra in the mouse nursery.

Arthur Take heart, Merlin. With both you and my trusted sword, Excalibur, at my side, I need fear no evil.

Merlin I hope you are right, Arthur. But I sense danger.

Merlin vanishes in a swirl of smoke. Sir Accolon shudders.

Accolon I am also glad, my lord, that the powers of the sorceror are on our side. Sometimes they chill me to the bone!

Arthur We shall certainly be chilled to the bone unless we find shelter. It is almost night.

Narrator *Suddenly, strangely, the mist closes all around. Then, through the gloom, a ship slowly appears, floating silently across the lake towards them.*

Accolon My lord! Whence came this vessel? The lake was empty, of that I am certain!

Arthur I cannot tell whence it comes, but it is most welcome. *(Calls)* Hallo! Hallo!

Accolon Be vigilant, sire. Remember the words of the wise magician.

Arthur Calm yourself, old friend. The ship itself is no danger. And if hoardes of warriors or a fire-belching dragon should emerge from within, then we shall deal with them. *(He taps the sword at his side)* We have defence enough for any man.

Narrator *As the ship reaches the shore, two female figures emerge from the ship and step down onto dry land. It is the evil Morgan le Fay and her servant, but both are heavily disguised.*

Servant Have we found two weary travellers?

Morgan What luck that we should come this way.

Arthur Luck indeed, my lady! We seek shelter from the night's cold.

Morgan le Fay snaps her fingers. Her servant bows and hurries back inside the ship.

Morgan And food and drink, no doubt? You are welcome to share what supplies we have.

Accolon *(whispers)* Be wary, my lord.

Arthur Of two young maidens bearing food? Come now, Sir Accolon, you are far too suspicious.

The servant reappears with a large tray, on which are food and two metal goblets.

Servant Why not drink a toast, good gentlemen? Here is wine from foreign lands, the finest you'll ever have tasted.

Arthur and Sir Accolon each take a goblet and hold it aloft.

Arthur Your good health, ladies!

They drink. Then they drop the goblets and collapse to the ground, unconscious.

Narrator *The wine is drugged. Both Arthur and Sir Accolon are now in the deepest of sleeps.*

Morgan le Fay removes her disguise and kneels beside Arthur. She moves his inert head from side to side with her forefinger.

Morgan Sleep well, half-brother. For in the morning, you die.

Woodland, as before. It is morning. Morgan le Fay and her servant are standing over Arthur and Sir Accolon, who are still asleep on the ground.

Narrator *Soon the effects of the drugged wine will wear off. Morgan le Fay prepares to hatch her murderous plot.*

Servant Why couldn't we put them to the sword as they sleep, my lady?

Morgan Because, fool, the whole of Camelot would then cry out for vengeance on their murderers. This way, one of them will kill the other. You and I can vanish from the scene, all unsuspected.

Narrator *Morgan and her servant drag their victims to separate spots, so that neither can see nor hear the other. Morgan replaces Excalibur with another sword, then puts Excalibur into the hand of Sir Accolon. As the men begin to stir, helmets are placed over their heads to obscure their faces. Then Morgan and her servant adopt their disguises once more.*

Servant *(to Sir Accolon)* Oh, help us, good sir knight! My lady is menaced by the dastardly Sir Damas!

Accolon *(groaning)* My head's in a spin! But never fear, my lady, I shall protect you!

He staggers to his feet. So does Arthur, who then spots Sir Accolon advancing towards him from the distance.

Arthur Who is that rogue I see?

Morgan It is the dastardly Sir Damas, sire! He is threatening to behead us all!

Arthur Fear not, lady. With Excalibur in my hand, none shall prevail against me.

He draws the sword Morgan gave him. Sir Accolon bears down on Arthur, wielding Excalibur.

Accolon Menace a kind and charming lady, would you? Prepare to die, fiend!

Arthur The only blood spilt this day will be yours, o beheading monster!

Narrator *They fight fiercely. Meanwhile, Morgan and her servant watch the battle from the shadows.*

Servant What if the King should kill Sir Accolon?

Morgan That won't happen, idiot. Sir Accolon holds Excalibur. Arthur is sure to be defeated, and once he is dead, I shall claim his throne.

Narrator *Arthur and Sir Accolon fight on. Then, with a mighty blow, Sir Accolon thrusts Excalibur through Arthur's shoulder. Arthur falls, badly wounded.*

Servant You are right, lady! He dies! He dies!

Merlin rushes in, arms flung wide.

Merlin Not this day!

Merlin takes off Sir Accolon's helmet.

Arthur Sir Accolon! You traitor!

Accolon You dare impugn my name? The devil take you, beast!

Arthur removes his helmet. Sir Accolon cries out and drops to his knees.

Accolon My lord! I was cruelly deceived! I thought you were Sir Damas!

Morgan *(to servant)* Time for us to depart, I think.

Merlin You shall go nowhere, evil ones.

He holds up a hand. Morgan and her servant find themselves rooted to the spot. Merlin crouches at Arthur's side.

Arthur How came you here, Merlin?

Merlin I warned you of trouble, but I know you of old. I knew you would not heed my advice. I have travelled through the night to foil the plot of these so-called ladies.

He holds up a hand again. Morgan and her servant tear off their disguises.

Arthur Morgan le Fay! My own half-sister schemed to have me killed!

Accolon How could I have been so foolish?

Merlin You are not to blame, friend. These harpies preyed on the valour that is in both your hearts. We shall take the King to a nearby abbey. There his wounds shall be tended and he may rest.

Morgan Rest until my revenge shall destroy him!

Merlin Be gone! I shall transport you many miles away from here!

With a single gesture from Merlin, Morgan and her servant vanish from sight in a swirl of smoke.

Narrator *And so Merlin saves King Arthur's life. The three friends then travel to the abbey, hidden deep in the woods. So deeply is it hidden, even Merlin is sure that Morgan le Fay can never find it. In this, however, he is mistaken.*

A bed chamber in the abbey. Heavy wooden shutters cover a window. A storm rages outside. Enter Arthur, with his shoulder bandaged, followed by Merlin and Sir Accolon.

Narrator *Once King Arthur's wounds have been attended to, the three friends make plans for their return to Camelot.*

Accolon We must be vigilant, my lord, in case Morgan le Fay should strike at you again. Are the window shutters secure? Could she crawl into the chamber that way?

Arthur Calm yourself, Sir Accolon. We are all wise to her scheming now, and will be on our guard. The shutters are secure.

Merlin And outside the window runs a river of such vast breadth and fearful depth that no mortal could cross it undetected.

Accolon I do not want to leave you unattended, sire, but there are disputes at court which I must help to settle.

Merlin And I will accompany you, Sir Accolon. You may be in need of my magical protection when travelling by night in such a storm.

Accolon I thank you, sorceror. I only hope that the King will be safe here.

Arthur draws Excalibur from its scabbard, and flings the scabbard onto the covers of the bed.

Arthur Now Excalibur is returned to me, it shall not leave my side, not even as I sleep. Go to Camelot, friends, and when my wounds are healed and I have recovered, then I will make a triumphant return to the castle.

Accolon As you wish, my lord.

Narrator *Merlin and Sir Accolon leave for Camelot. Arthur wearily climbs into bed, tightly clutching Excalibur to his chest. For some moments, all that can be heard are the wind and rain outside the abbey.*

Arthur is asleep. The door to the chamber opens slowly, and Morgan enters, disguised as a nun. She quickly removes the disguise.

Morgan Thought yourself safe from me, did you? Sleeping like a baby. You do not deserve to be King. While I, by means of cunning and guile, shall destroy you and so prove myself a worthy Queen.

She approaches the bed.

Morgan Alas, he sleeps with Excalibur in his grasp! The weakling!

She spots the scabbard on the bed covers and snatches it at once.

Morgan Ah, luck is still on my side! Destroy the scabbard of Excalibur and the protection it gives him will be no more. But how can I put it beyond his reach forever?

Narrator *Morgan flings open the shutters at the window. Wind and rain blast in. With a howl of triumph, she hurls the scabbard through the window and it splashes into the depths of the river. Arthur is woken by the sudden noise, and leaps out of bed, Excalibur at the ready. He notices at once that the scabbard has gone.*

Arthur Is there no end to your treachery, Morgan le Fay?

Morgan Not while you live and I am denied the crown, half-brother!

Arthur Where is the scabbard?

Morgan Lost! For all eternity! Poor, poor Arthur, thou must do without its protection from now on.

She runs from the chamber. Arthur follows.

Narrator *King Arthur runs out into the night, chasing the evil Morgan le Fay. He is sure that he can catch her, even in the darkness, and the wind, and the rain. But he has forgotten that her magical powers are second only to Merlin's. She turns herself into a rock, which Arthur simply runs past, never realising it is Morgan. He returns to Camelot in the bitterest of moods.*

SCENE FOUR

Camelot. Arthur is seated on a large wooden throne. Merlin stands at his side. Enter Sir Accolon.

Narrator *Some time passes before Morgan le Fay dares to make another attempt on the life of King Arthur. One day, news reaches the King that Morgan's servant has appeared at the gates of Camelot.*

Accolon I come to tell you that Morgan's servant is asking for permission to speak with you. I presume I should send the girl running for the hills?

Arthur No, wait. What is your opinion, Merlin?

Merlin Your half-sister would have to be very brazen indeed to send a servant to kill you in your own castle, when surrounded by your court.

Arthur I agree. And as King, I should set an example to my people, one of tolerance and forgiveness. I shall hear what the servant has to say.

Accolon *(reluctantly)* Very well, my lord.

Narrator *A few minutes later, Sir Accolon returns, accompanied by Morgan's servant, who is carrying a glittering, bejewelled robe. She bows before the King.*

Servant Your majesty, I thank you for granting me this audience.

Arthur Tell me your purpose in attending my court.

Servant I bring you this robe, as a gift from my mistress, Morgan le Fay.

Accolon A gift? From that evil creature?

Arthur We will hear her out, Sir Accolon. *(To the servant)* If your mistress were to give me a gift, I would expect a bottle of poison, or a deadly serpent. Why would she present me with this finery?

Servant Your majesty, I bring a message of sincere sorrow. My mistress has repented of all the evil she has done to you in the past. Now she weeps day and night over the harm she has caused. She is changed. She hopes that this robe will demonstrate her true feelings.

Merlin And a wondrous robe it is. Will you put it on, girl, so that we can see it to best advantage?

Servant No! I mean, sir, that it is meant only for the King. A mere servant like me could never presume to –

Merlin Come, come. The King wishes to see it in all its glory. Is that not right, Arthur?

Arthur I am guided by your wisdom, Merlin.

Merlin takes the robe from the servant and goes to place it on her shoulders. She leaps away in fright.

Servant It is for the King alone! My mistress commands it!

Narrator *Merlin throws the robe to Sir Accolon, who wraps it around the servant before she can react. Suddenly, with a scream, she bursts into flames. In seconds, both the servant and the robe are reduced to ashes.*

Sir Accolon *(astounded)* What wickedness is here? These flames were meant for you, my lord.

Arthur *(enraged)* So this is the love my evil sister bears me!

Merlin Without your scabbard you are vulnerable. Henceforth, you must be always on your guard against her.

Arthur I will do more than that. Good knights, take heed of my vow. I hereby renounce my fiendish half-sister. From this day on, Morgan le Fay is banished, forever, from my heart and from Camelot!

Did Arthur exist? No one knows for sure. We do know that the Ancient Britons had to fight off the northern Picts, the Irish, and Saxon invaders. The Britons were led by a chieftain, a hero of his time – could this have been Arthur?

In *The Scheming of Morgan le Fay*, Arthur narrowly escapes death more than once at the hands of his evil half-sister, Morgan. Luckily for him, Merlin is on hand to keep him safe.

Arthur

Arthur is one of the great British folk heroes – noble, honest and loyal. He is headstrong and careless at times, but his heart is in the right place! Merlin often appears from nowhere to help Arthur at critical times.

Morgan le Fay

Morgan is Arthur's mother's child from an earlier marriage. She is a wicked enchantress with powers to match Merlin's. Legend has it that it was Merlin who originally developed Morgan's powers as a healer. However, her jealousy of Arthur has turned these powers from good to evil.

Camelot

Camelot is most likely a legendary version of Cadbury castle, near Glastonbury in Somerset.

READY, STEADY, ACT!

Now that you have read this play, why not perform it for an audience and bring the story alive for them?

CHOOSING THE PARTS

Choose who will play each part by holding auditions.

- The narrator is a clear speaker who talks directly to the audience.
- Merlin, the magician, is mysterious and aloof.
- King Arthur is a strong and chivalrous knight, but he is not good at taking advice.
- Sir Accolon is a loyal, dutiful knight.
- Morgan le Fay is a beautiful and wicked woman, with magical powers.
- Morgan's servant does her lady's bidding without question.

Choose some typical lines from each character and see who is best at saying them.

SETTING THE SCENE

The scenes are set in a gloomy wood by a lake, a bed chamber and Camelot. You could use lighting, some props or some scenery to show this. It can be as simple or as complicated as you have time for.

Did you know...?

Did you know that the name Morgan le Fay means 'Morgan the fairy'.

WHAT YOU WILL NEED

Costumes

Unless you have costumes you will have to improvise. A simple way would be to dress in black and add crown, swords, cloaks, false beards or face paints. Can you use colour to represent good and bad characters?

Props

Make a props list using the text. You will need a throne, which could be a decorated chair. You could make the sword Excalibur and its scabbard, or use a toy sword. How will you manage the helmets?

Sound effects

The storm could be represented with musical instruments and voices. You could use some red cloth for the burning cloak, or you could do this off-stage. Plenty of loud screaming will help make this scene believable! You may need some extra knights and ladies on stage to watch the dramatic scene in Camelot.

SPEAKING AND MOVING

Speaking

The speech in this play is melodramatic. Be careful not to make the lines sound funny – you don't want people to laugh!

Moving

The first sight of Merlin is as a ghost. How will he move to make this spooky? He is very powerful. He only has to raise his hand and Morgan is rooted to the spot.

Take care in the fighting scenes. Use slow motion and careful planning to keep safe.

There is some fast action in the final scene when Merlin throws the cloak to Sir Accolon, who wraps it round the girl before she can get away.

What next?

Why not

- Improvise a magical duel of spells between Merlin and Morgan le Fay.
- Make a comic strip of the story.